Art and Culture

Dancing
Around the World

Comparing Groups

Linda Claire

There are more shoes than tutus.

Russia

ballet

There are fewer dresses than jackets.

Cuba

salsa

There are the same number of skirts and cloaks.

New Zealand

haka

There are more dresses than vests.

Ireland

Irish jig

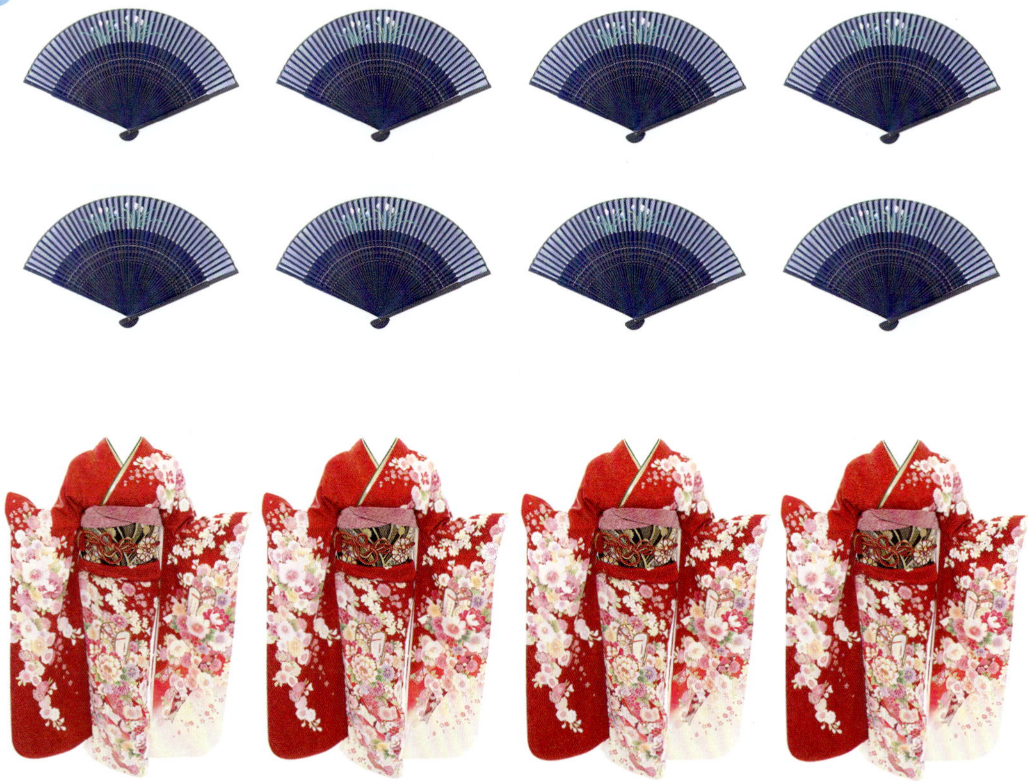

There are fewer robes than fans.

Japan

kabuki

There are the same number of masks and drums. The numbers are equal.

Nigeria

Gelede

There are fewer hats than shoes.

United States

break dancing

Problem Solving

Rosa has many things for dancing. Count and compare them.

1. Are there more tutus or shoes?

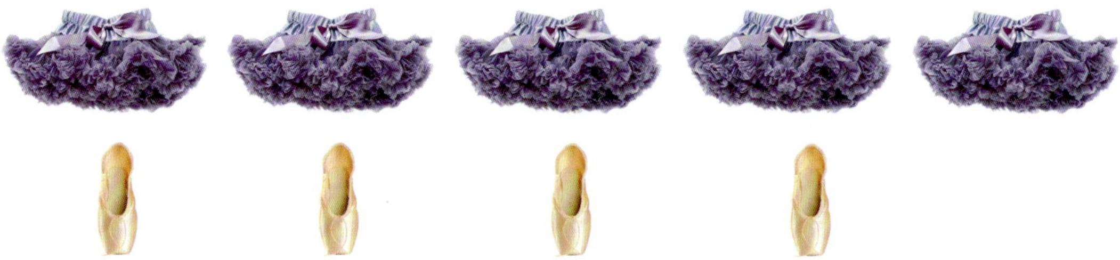

2. Are there fewer fans or umbrellas?

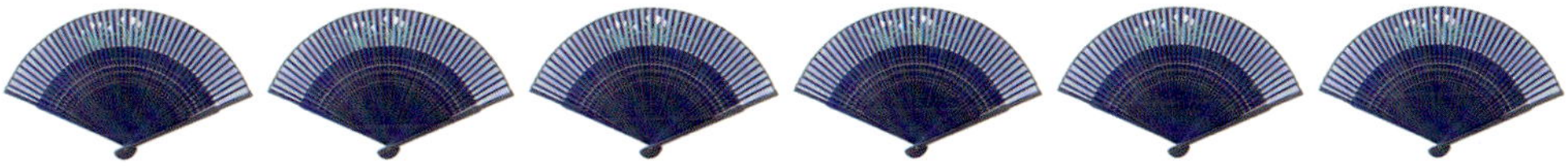

3. How did you compare the things in the groups?

Answer Key

1. tutus
2. umbrellas
3. Answers will vary but may include matching or counting.

Consultants

Nicole Belasco, M.Ed.
Kindergarten Teacher, Colonial School District

Colleen Pollitt, M.A.Ed.
Math Support Teacher, Howard County Public Schools

Publishing Credits

Rachelle Cracchiolo, M.S.Ed., *Publisher*
Conni Medina, M.A.Ed., *Managing Editor*
Dona Herweck Rice, *Series Developer*
Emily R. Smith, M.A.Ed., *Series Developer*
Diana Kenney, M.A.Ed., NBCT, *Content Director*
June Kikuchi, *Content Director*
Véronique Bos, *Creative Director*
Robin Erickson, *Art Director*
Stacy Monsman, M.A., and Karen Malaska, M.Ed., *Editors*
Michelle Jovin, M.A., *Associate Editor*
Fabiola Sepulveda, *Graphic Designer*

Image Credits: p.6 (top) 3C Stock/Alamy; p.6 (bottom) National Museum of New Zealand Te Papa Tongarewa; p.7 Jack Grieve/Alamy; p.12 (top) PRAWNS/Alamy; p.13 Danita Delimont/Alamy; all other images from iStock and/or Shutterstock.

Library of Congress Cataloging-in-Publication Data

Names: Claire, Linda, author.
Title: Art and culture. Dancing around the world / Linda Claire.
Other titles: Dancing around the world
Description: Huntington Beach, CA : Teacher Created Materials, 2018. | Audience: K to Grade 3. |
Identifiers: LCCN 2017059893 (print) | LCCN 2018014615 (ebook) | ISBN 9781480759527 (e-book) | ISBN 9781425856144 (pbk.)
Subjects: LCSH: Dance--Juvenile literature.
Classification: LCC GV1596.5 (ebook) | LCC GV1596.5 .R53 2018 (print) | DDC 792.8--dc23
LC record available at https://lccn.loc.gov/2017059893

Teacher Created Materials
5301 Oceanus Drive
Huntington Beach, CA 92649-1030
www.tcmpub.com

ISBN 978-1-4258-5614-4

Printed in China
51497